Garbage Collectors

Julie Murray

Abdo Kids Junior
is an Imprint of Abdo Kids
abdopublishing.com

Abdo
MY COMMUNITY: JOBS
Kids

abdopublishing.com

Published by Abdo Kids, a division of ABDO, P.O. Box 398166, Minneapolis, Minnesota 55439.
Copyright © 2019 by Abdo Consulting Group, Inc. International copyrights reserved in all countries.
No part of this book may be reproduced in any form without written permission from the publisher.
Abdo Kids Junior™ is a trademark and logo of Abdo Kids.

Printed in the United States of America, North Mankato, Minnesota.

052018

092018

THIS BOOK CONTAINS
RECYCLED MATERIALS

Photo Credits: Glow Images, iStock, Shutterstock

Production Contributors: Teddy Borth, Jennie Forsberg, Grace Hansen

Design Contributors: Christina Doffing, Candice Keimig, Dorothy Toth

Library of Congress Control Number: 2017960553
Publisher's Cataloging-in-Publication Data

Names: Murray, Julie, author.

Title: Garbage collectors / by Julie Murray.

Description: Minneapolis, Minnesota : Abdo Kids, 2019. | Series: My community: Jobs |
    Includes glossary, index and online resources (page 24).

Identifiers: ISBN 9781532107887 (lib.bdg.) | ISBN 9781532108860 (ebook) |
    ISBN 9781532109355 (Read-to-me ebook)

Subjects: LCSH: Sanitation workers--Garbage collectors--Juvenile literature. | Occupations--Careers—
    Jobs--Juvenile literature. | Community life--Juvenile literature.

Classification: DDC 628.442--dc23

Table of Contents

Garbage Collectors

Here comes a big truck. Who is driving? The garbage collector!

They help keep the city clean.

The driver sits in the cab.

It is in the front.

Nico pulls a lever. The trash is lifted. It goes into the bin.

Some do it by hand. Joe lifts the garbage can.

Amy pushes the button.

The trash is crushed.

Now more can fit.

NOT FOR LIFTING

15

They follow a route. It is the same each week.

They stop at businesses.

They stop at houses too.

The truck is full. Time to go to the dump.

A Garbage Collector's Tools

garbage truck

reflective vest

route

trash cans

Glossary

cab
the front of a truck where the driver sits.

crush
to break down into small pieces by pressing very hard.

lever
a handle used to control a machine.

route
a road of travel from one place to the next that a garbage truck follows every week.

Index

Abdo Kids ONLINE
FREE! ONLINE MULTIMEDIA RESOURCES

Visit **abdokids.com** and use this code to access crafts, games, videos, and more!

Abdo Kids Code: **MGK7887**